First Facts®

D0010367

The Middle Ages

# Medieval Arms and Armor

by Jim Whiting

**Consultant:**
James Masschaele
Associate Professor of Medieval History
Rutgers University
New Brunswick, New Jersey

Capstone
press®

Mankato, Minnesota

First Facts is published by Capstone Press,
151 Good Counsel Drive, P.O. Box 669, Mankato, Minnesota 56002.
www.capstonepress.com

*Library of Congress Cataloging-in-Publication Data*
Whiting, Jim, 1943–
    Medieval arms and armor / by Jim Whiting.
    p. cm. — (First facts. The Middle Ages)
    Includes bibliographical references and index.
    Summary: "Describes the weapons and defenses used in the Middle Ages" —
Provided by publisher.
    ISBN-13: 978-1-4296-2270-7 (hardcover)
    ISBN-10: 1-4296-2270-9 (hardcover)
    1. Weapons — History — Juvenile literature. 2. Armor, Medieval — History —
Juvenile literature. I. Title. II. Series.
U800.W54 2009
623.4'41 — dc22
                                        2008032332

**Editorial Credits**
Megan Schoeneberger, editor; Kim Brown, designer; Marcie Spence, photo researcher

**Photo Credits**
Alamy/David Young-Wolff, 20; Alamy/Holmes Garden Photo, 16; Alamy/ilian studio, 12; Alamy/
Tony Cordoza, 9; Art Resource, N.Y./ The Metropolitan Museum of Art, 18; Capstone Press/Karon
Dubke, 21; Getty Images Inc./Fritz Goro/Time Life Pictures, 10; Getty Images Inc./Hulton Archive,
1; iStockphoto/Dusko Jovic, cover (left); Private Collection, © Look and Learn/The Bridgeman Art
Library International, 13; Private Collection/The Bridgeman Art Library International, 5; Regional Art
Museum, Kaluga/The Bridgeman Art Library International, 6; Shutterstock/Mikhail Olykainen, 17;
Shutterstock/Mityukhin Oleg Petrovich, 7; Shutterstock/Sibrikov Valery, cover (right); Shutterstock/
Tatarszkij, 15

Essential content terms are **bold** and are defined at the bottom of the page where they first appear.

# Table of Contents

# Medieval Battles

In medieval times, wars were as normal as eating and sleeping. Governments were weak. Rulers couldn't enforce laws very well. Landowners called **nobles** took laws into their own hands. Their armies often attacked each other. Fighters needed arms and armor to protect themselves.

noble — a wealthy person of high rank

# Arms and Armor of the Middle Ages
## Europe
### 476 – 1500

armor

long bow

sword

shield

lance

cross bow

chain mail

battle ax

spear

polearm

## Medieval Fact!
Arms and armor were similar across Europe throughout the Middle Ages.

5

# Chain Mail

Early knights wore heavy **chain mail** when they fought. This iron armor weighed about 50 pounds (23 kilograms). It protected knights from cuts. But it didn't soften hits from heavy weapons. Chain mail also fell apart easily. It often rusted and was hard to clean.

**chain mail** — metal armor made of thousands of tiny iron rings linked together

# Cloth Armor

Foot soldiers couldn't afford metal armor. Many wore cloth armor instead. It was much cheaper but not very helpful. Still, it was better than no armor at all. Two layers of heavy cloth were sewn together. Then men stuffed it with wool, cotton, or rags. Fighting in cloth armor was like exercising in a heavy winter jacket.

## Medieval Fact!

Only a few men could become knights. Almost all knights came from wealthy families.

# Knights in Shining Armor

In the 1200s, knights began wearing armor made of solid metal plates. A plate armor suit weighed about the same as chain mail. It had more than 24 pieces. Each piece protected one part of a knight's body. Joints bent to let knights move.

## *Medieval Fact!*
Plate armor was polished or painted so it wouldn't rust.

helmet

shield

sword

# Don't Lose Your Head!

A knight's helmet was very important. It covered his entire head. Thick padding softened the blows of weapons. Slits in the front let him see out and breathe. Helmets were hot, heavy, and uncomfortable to wear. Knights usually waited until just before a battle began to put them on.

## Medieval Fact!

Eye slits in helmets were very small. Knights couldn't see much. Helmets fit so tightly that the knights could barely hear.

# The Knight's Weapons

A sword was the knight's main weapon. Swords were very expensive. They were made of iron or steel. Knights used swords to slash at enemies as they thundered past on horses.

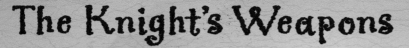

### Medieval Fact!
Knights also carried battle-axes. These heavy weapons had sharp, curved iron blades on wooden handles. Battle-axes were nicknamed "bonecrushers" because they made horrible wounds.

Knights also fought with lances. These long wooden poles had sharp metal tips. Knights held them next to their bodies as they charged into battle.

# Fighting on Foot

Foot soldiers had several weapons. Crossbows were small bows attached to a heavy piece of wood. They fired metal darts with great force. Spears had wooden handles and sharp steel points. Polearms had cutting or slashing weapons at the end of a long pole.

## Medieval Fact!

Foot soldiers tried to knock knights off their horses. The weight of a knight's armor made it hard to stand up again. The soldiers stabbed knights through the joints in their armor.

crossbow

# Medieval Machine Guns

The English longbow was the machine gun of medieval times. It was made of wood and stood 6 feet (1.8 meters) high. Arrows could hit targets more than two football fields away. A few hundred **archers** could shoot thousands of arrows every minute.

**archer** — a person who shoots with a bow and arrow

# Shields

Most soldiers carried shields. Shields were usually made of several thin layers of wood glued together. Some shields were small and round. Others were shaped like kites and stood several feet (meters) high.

## Medieval Fact!

When knights began wearing full armor, many stopped carrying shields. Their armor gave them enough protection.

# The End of Armor

Guns changed the way that battles were fought. Armor thick enough to stop bullets was too heavy to wear. Knights no longer fought on battlefields. But their arms and armor didn't go away. Today you can see these weapons in museums. They give an interesting look into medieval times.

# Amazing but True!

In the Middle Ages, horses wore armor called barding. One piece protected the horse's face and ears. Another piece covered its neck. More armor protected the animal's chest and back legs. But horses couldn't be completely armored. Their front legs and stomach were not protected.

# Try It Out:
## Knight's Helmet

You can look and feel like a knight of the Middle Ages with your own helmet. You'll learn how hard it was for knights to see. And it will probably get pretty warm inside after a few minutes.

### What You Need

- two sheets of lightweight cardboard
- duct tape
- a craft knife or scissors
- aluminum foil

### What You Do

1. Have an adult roll one sheet of cardboard into a tube that fits over your head. It should fit snugly but not too tight. Tape the tube together with duct tape.
2. Cut a circle from the other piece of cardboard to put on top of the helmet. Use a few pieces of tape to hold it in place.
3. Cut a narrow opening so you can see out.
4. Cover the helmet with aluminum foil. You can also punch some small holes to make it easier to breathe.

# Glossary

**archer** (AR-chuhr) — a person who shoots at targets with a bow and arrow

**barding** (BAHRD-ing) — the armor worn by knights' horses

**battle-ax** (BAT-uhl-aks) — a weapon consisting of a wooden handle with a heavy, sharp blade on one end

**chain mail** (CHAYN MAYL) — armor made up of thousands of tiny iron rings linked together

**noble** (NOH-buhl) — a person of high rank or birth

# Read More

**Doeden, Matt.** *Weapons of the Middle Ages.* Weapons of War. Mankato, Minn.: Capstone Press, 2009.

**MacDonald, Fiona.** *You Wouldn't Want to Be a Medieval Knight: Armor You'd Rather Not Wear.* New York: Franklin Watts, 2004.

**Murrell, Deborah.** *Weapons.* Medieval Warfare. Pleasantville, N.Y.: Gareth Stevens, 2009.

**Weintraub, Aileen.** *Knights: Warriors of the Middle Ages.* Way of the Warrior. New York: Children's Press, 2005.

# Internet Sites

FactHound offers a safe, fun way to find educator-approved Internet sites related to this book.

Here's what you do:
1. Visit *www.facthound.com*
2. Choose your grade level.
3. Begin your search.

This book's ID number is 9781429622707.

FactHound will fetch the best sites for you!

# Index